for

Chris Blanchard

Whose Spirit Triumphs

Dale Chihuly
Bellagio
Fiori di Como
Las Vegas, Nevada
1998

PORTLAND PRESS ~ SEATTLE

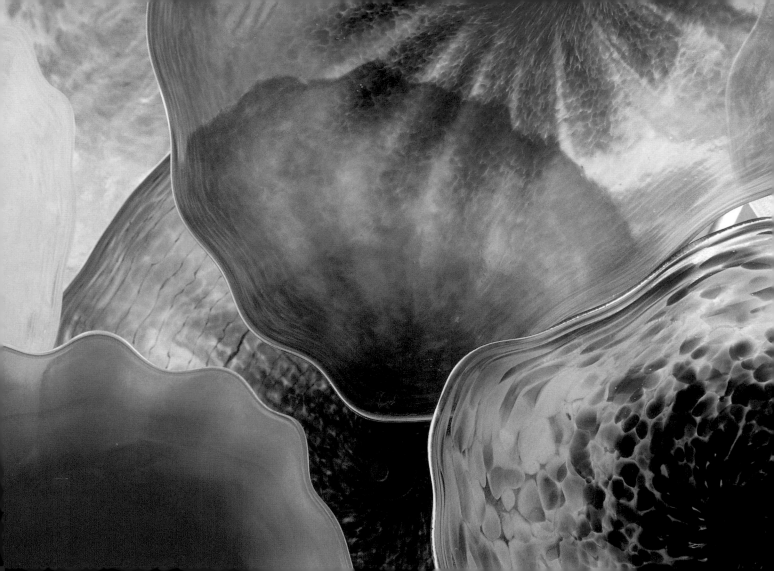

How is this project unique?

First of all the scale, and secondly, the number of talented people who make up the team: glassblowers, architects, engineers, shippers, installers, and fabricators—over 100 in all. It took about 10,000 pounds of steel for the armature and some 40,000 pounds of hand-blown glass—over 2,000 pieces positioned fifteen to twenty-five feet overhead. It also demanded an entirely new type of hardware to attach the glass to the structure.

Fiori di Como is your largest single work—2,100 square feet, some 2,000 pieces of glass. The deadline (opening night of Bellagio) was one challenge, but what was the greatest creative challenge for you?

Everything about *Fiori di Como* was new—the scale, the armature, and the glass. First I had to develop the way the ceiling would look—the depth, new glass forms, the technique for holding the glass, all the safety issues involving suspending a 40,000-pound artwork overhead. We started by constructing four prototypes in my studio for Elaine and Steve Wynn to see. After Steve made three trips to Seattle, we finally decided on the right look for the project—one that had ten feet of depth and required a very complicated steel armature that comes down like branches of a tree. Color was the most difficult aesthetic challenge, and the structure was the most difficult technical challenge.

Why Fiori di Como?

I'm amazed at what people find in my work, and I don't like
to limit what you see with a title. For me titles are very
difficult, and I don't usually even think in terms of a theme
when I'm creating a sculpture. Once it's finished I'll come
up with a title, but one person might see flowers, another
something from the sea or something from a dream. Bellagio
was inspired by the hotel on Lake Como, and I wanted to use
the lake in the title—it's so romantic. I used the word *fiori*
(flowers), but everybody sees something different.

Can a work be too colorful? How do you set the palette?

I don't know if something can be too colorful. Color is one
of the great properties of glass and is more intense in glass
than any other material. Imagine entering Chartres Cathedral
and looking up at the Rose Window: you can see a one-inch
square of ruby red glass from 300 feet away. In *Fiori di Como*
I wanted to use a lot of color but ended up utilizing only about
40 of the 350 colors in my palette. I made the color appear
random, yet organized as you might find in nature.

DALE CHIHULY, 1998

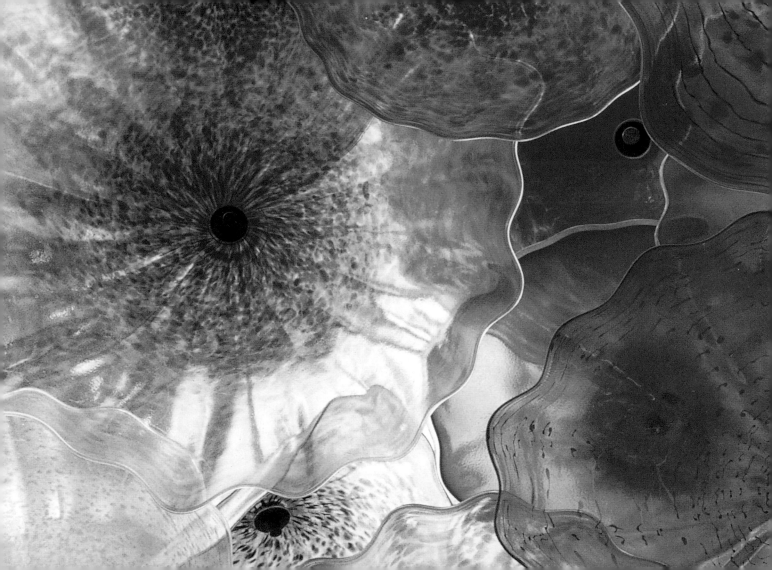

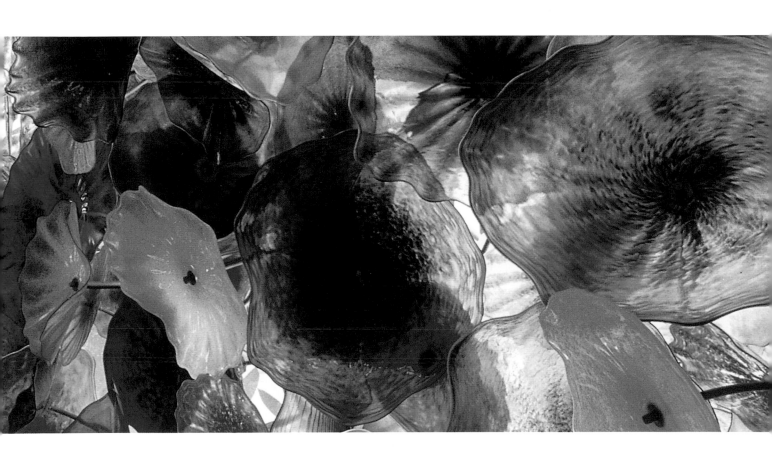

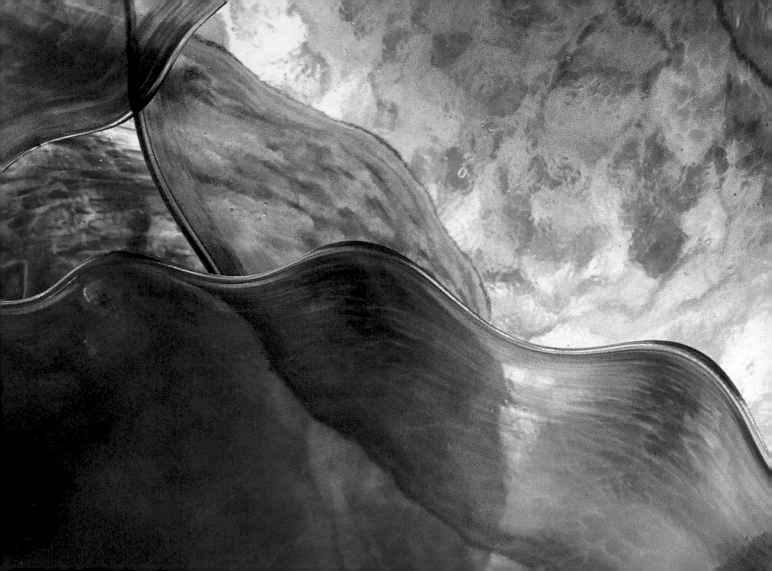

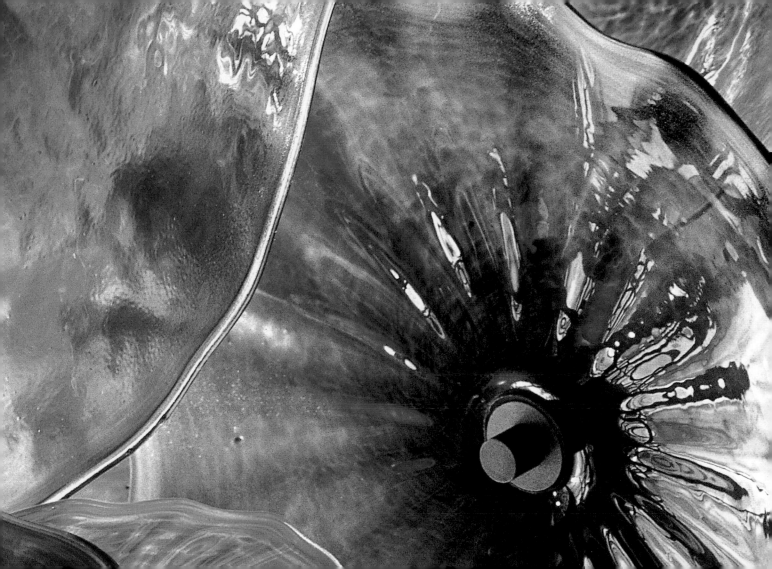

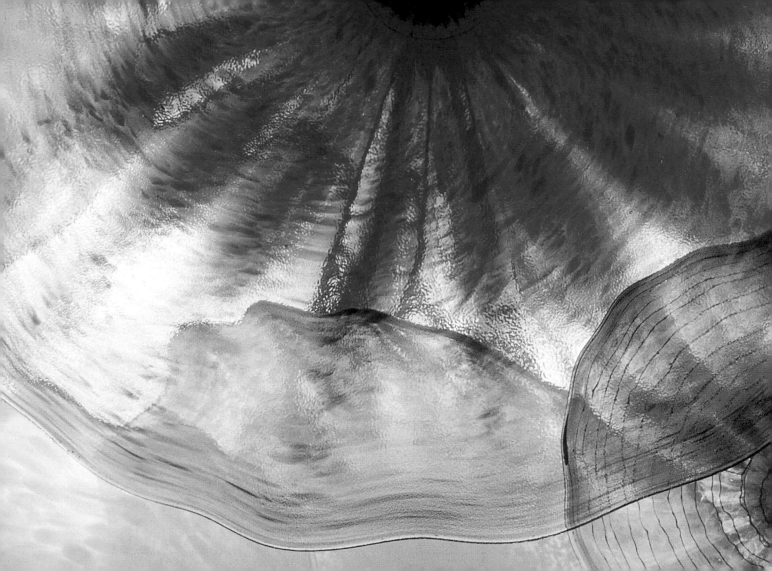

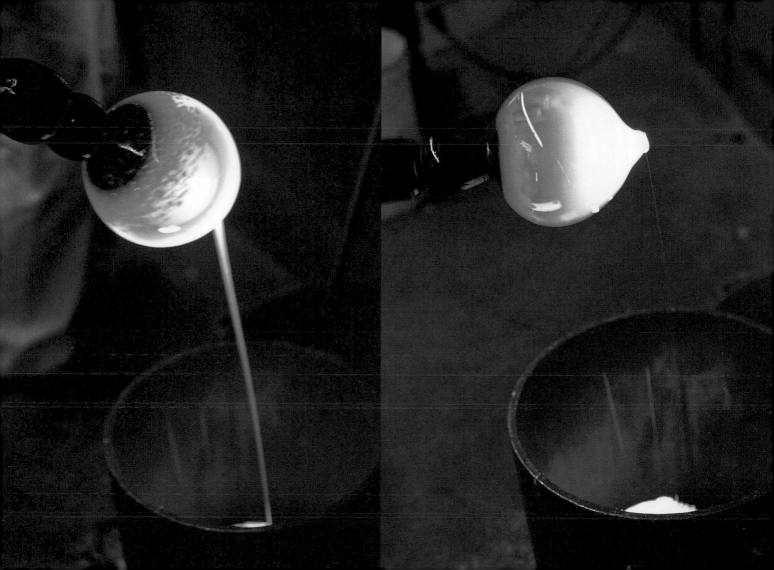

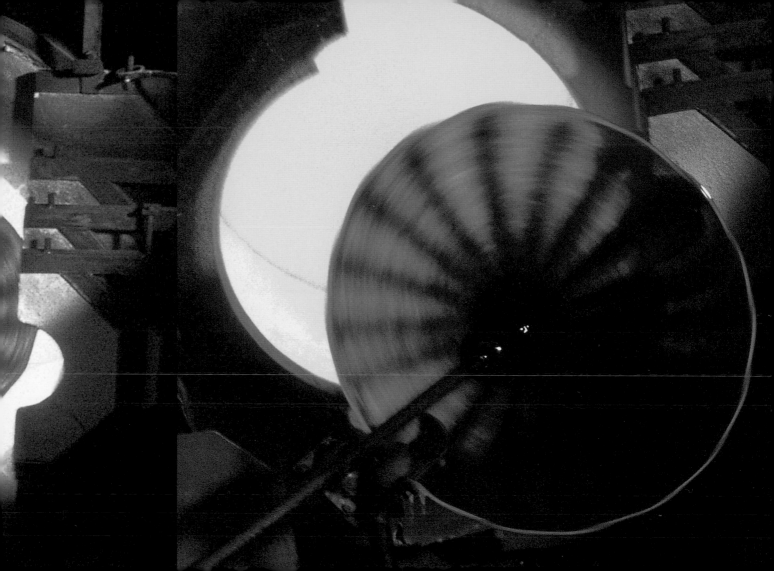

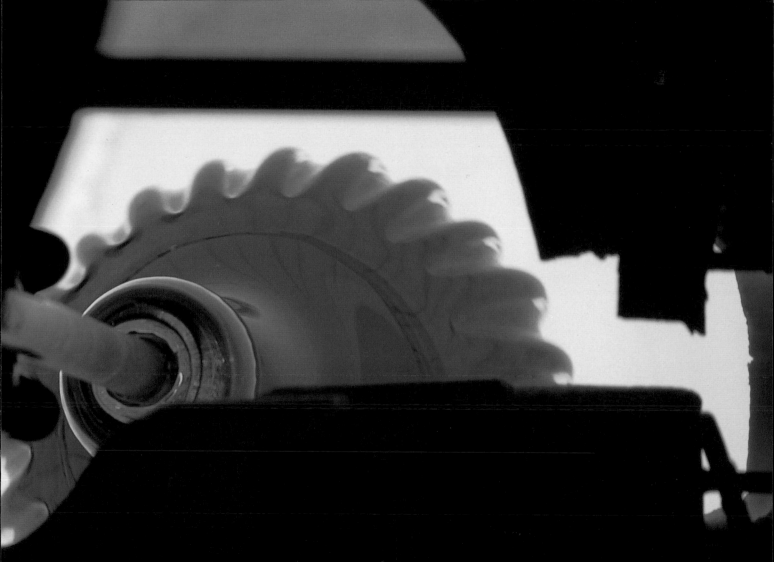

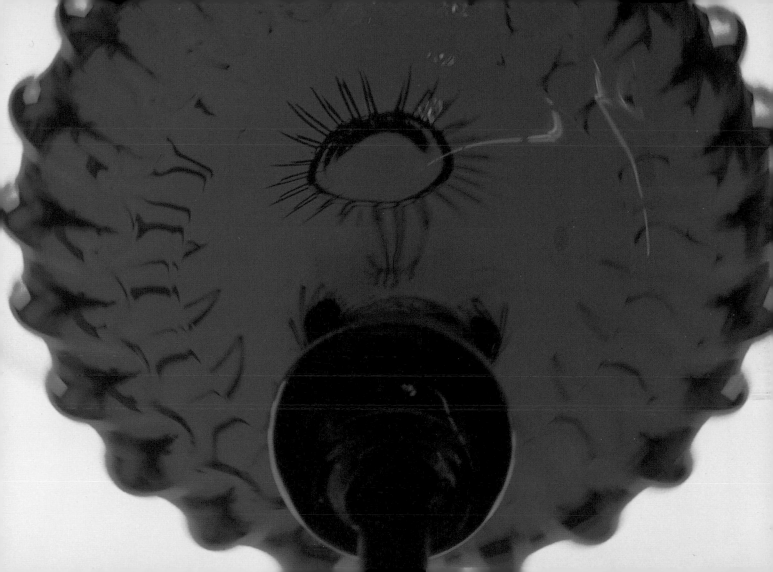

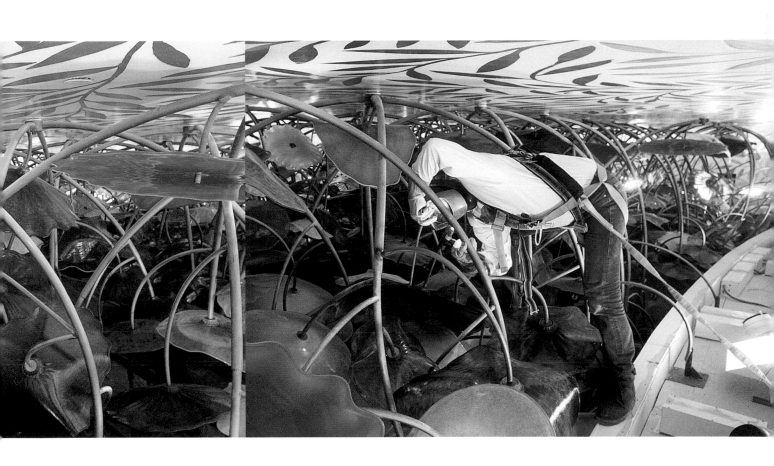

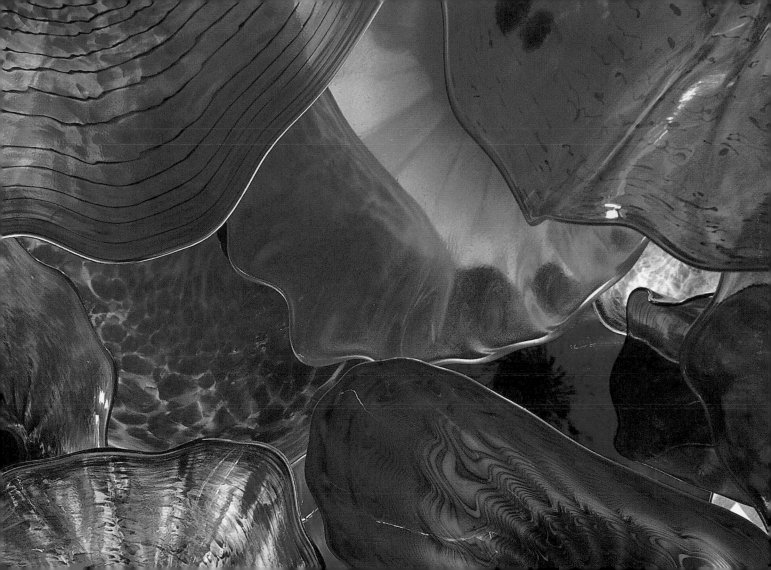

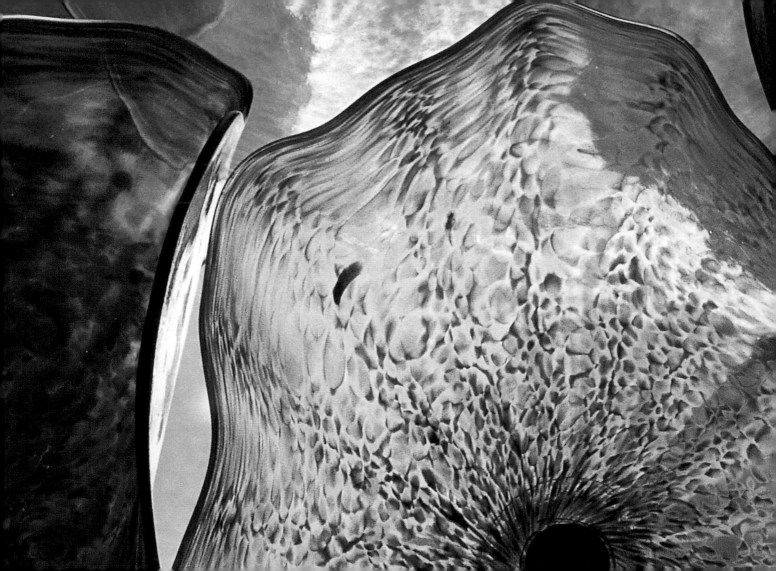

CHIHULY STUDIO 509 NE NORTHLAKE WAY SEATTLE, WA 98105
TEL: 206 632 8707 FAX: 206 632-8825

Dear Steve.
It was great to watch you
in action & to help in some small
way with the design of what will
be the greatest, grandest hotel in
the world! I'm here in room E9
'til tomorrow morning if there's
anything else I can do. Sitting
here thinking about the lobby
& making a few sketches.
this one's ceiling is too high
but it gives a feeling
of how the ceiling
might be.
Thanks for
the great
evening
Dale

074

page 2 of 3

Job 6
1997

Bellagio

073

What a Team
Thanx Everybody!

Cinly
Seattle Dec. '98

TEAM CHIHULY

Heather Abbott
Debra Abney
April Adams
Zack Almont
Parks Anderson
Ralph Atkins
Eric Augino
Tom Barnes
Steve Barrett
Theresa Batty
Jeff Bender
David Bennett
John Bennett
Kai-Uwe Bergmann
Chris Blanchard
Elaine Bowers
Belinda Bowling
Roger Bransteitter
Michael Bray
Diane Caillier
Blaze Campbell
Jean-Pierre Canlis
Greg Carlow
Jason Carlow
Scott Carlson
Shaun Chappell
Kim Christiansen
Ken Clark
Steve Cochran
Heath Conner
Tim Conner
Steven Cornett

Jack Crane
Anna Katherine
  Curfman
Patricia Davidson
Joey DeCamp
Leigh Deckert
Mary DeCuzzi
Chase DeForest
Darin Denison
Carol DePelecyn
Nadege Desgenetez
Paul DeSomma
Romi Epstein
Bob Fair
Kent Faust
Jon Felix
Jeanne Marie Ferraro
Teresa Forrester
Michael Fox
Gabriel Garcia
Claire Garoutte
Jeff Gerber
Manisone Gipson
Bruce Greck
Kim Hall
Gary Hayden
James Hearsey
Noelle Higgins
Nathan Hoadley
Donald Hudgins
Karin Johnson
Russell Johnson

Bennett Jordan
Nichole Jose
Briahna Kalil
Chris Kaul
Radovan Klement
Wilbur Kelly
Mary Kilimann
Kalee Kirschenbaum
John Landon
Joel Langholz
Shelly Langton
Eileen Lannan
Tom Lind
Elizabeth Ling
Lisa MacDonald
Laurence Madrelle
Breta Malcolm
Duane Marsh
Ed McDonald
Mark McDonnell
Bennett McKnight
Rick McNett
Mitchell Minskoff
Joan Monetta
Jim Mongrain
Jason Mouer
Beverly Mundy
Ami Noss
Mark O'Neil
Carolynn O'Rourke
Patrick Orr
DJ Palin

Dennis Palin
Bob Park
Sarah Parker
Debbie Parmenter
Charles Parriott
Eric Pauli
Julie Poth
Michele Reilly
Thomas Reynolds
Annette Ringe
Teresa Rishel
Terry Rishel
Barry Rosen
Bryan Rubino
Michael Rydinski
Sean Salstrom
Ken Samuelsen
Patrick Sandstrom
David Schoales
Lisa Sears
Joanna Sikes
Daryl Smith
Megan Smith
Linda Snow
Dan Spitzer
Paula Stackpole
Robin Stark
Anna Starling
Christina Stein
Philip Stewart
Paula Stokes
James Sundstad

Michelle Swerland
Aarron Tate
Chuck Taylor
Mike Venema
Allen Vinup
David Walters
Jessica Wentworth
Eric Woll
Patsy Wooten
Thomas York
Veronika
  Zahradnikova
Kristen Zimmerman

This first edition of Chihuly: Bellagio is limited to 10,000 casebound copies. The photographers and videographers are Theresa Batty, Shaun Chappell, Claire Garoutte, Russell Johnson, Teresa Rishel, Terry Rishel, Ken Samuelsen, Philip Stewart and Thomas York.

Book design by Werkhaus, Seattle. The text is set in Mrs. Eaves. The photographs were reproduced using IPI process inks on NPI 157 gsm matt art paper.

Portland Press
Seattle, Washington
800 574-7272
www.portlandpress.net

Library of Congress Cataloging-in-Publication Data

Dale Chihuly/Bellagio
ISBN 1-57684-009-3
1. Chihuly, Dale 1941- —Criticism and interpretation.
2. Art glass—United States—History—20th century.
I. Title.

Published in 1999 by Portland Press, Seattle.
First edition